SIMPLE
JEWISH
COOKERY

COMPILED BY EDNA BEILENSON

AND DECORATED BY

RUTH MCCREA

Peter Pauper Press
MOUNT VERNON · NEW YORK

The Jewish Holidays

ROSH HASHONAH *(Tishri* 1, 2) The Jewish New Year, occurs in September or October.

YOM KIPPUR *(Tishri* 10) The Day of Atonement, occurs in September or October.

SUKKOS *(Tishri* 15-23) The Harvest Feast, occurs in October.

CHANUKAH *(Kislev* 25 — *Tebet* 2) The Feast of the Lights, or The Saving of the Temple, occurs in December.

PURIM *(Adar* 14) Festival of the Book of Esther, a Carnival and Masquerade, occurs in March.

PESACH, anglicized as Passover *(Nissan* 14-22) celebrates the freeing of the Israelites from bondage in Egypt, and occurs in April.

SHAVUOS *(Sivan* 6, 7) Birthday of the Torah, originally an agricultural feast celebrating the planting of the wheat, occurs in May or June.

SHABBOS, the Jewish Sabbath, is celebrated weekly from sundown on Friday to sundown on Saturday. In the orthodox tradition, it is a day given over entirely to devotion at the synagogue, and freedom from work. No cooking is allowed.

Sabbath

The observance of the Sabbath is one of the three positive commands in the Ten Commandments. The Sabbath begins with blessings over light and wine to give release, peace, gaiety, and lifted spirits.

Challah

1 cake yeast
2 teaspoons sugar
1¼ cups warm water
4½ cups sifted flour
2 teaspoons salt
2 eggs
2 tablespoons salad oil
1 egg yolk
4 tablespoons poppy seeds

Combine yeast, sugar and ¼ cup warm

5

water and let stand 5 minutes. Sift flour and salt into a bowl, making a well in center. Drop in eggs, oil, remaining water and yeast mixture. Work into the flour.

Knead on a floured surface until smooth and elastic. Place in a bowl and brush top with a little oil. Cover with towel, set in a warm place and let rise 1 hour. Punch down and cover again. Let rise until double in bulk.

Divide the dough into 3 equal parts. Between lightly floured hands roll the dough into 3 strips of equal length. Braid strips together and place in baking pan. Cover with towel and let rise until double in bulk. Brush with egg yolk and sprinkle with poppy seeds. Bake in 350° oven about 50 minutes or until brown.

Chopped Chicken Liver

½ cup shortening, or chicken fat
2 medium-size onions, sliced
1 pound chicken livers
2 eggs, hard-boiled
1½ teaspoons salt
¼ teaspoon pepper

Melt ¼ cup of shortening in a skillet. Add the onions. Sauté for 10 minutes, then remove and set aside. Melt the remaining ¼ cup of shortening in the same skillet. Sauté the livers in it for 10 minutes, stirring occasionally. Chop onions, livers, and eggs very fine in a wooden bowl. Add the salt and pepper and mix well. Chill.

Serve as an *hors d'oeuvre* with crackers, or as an appetizer on crisp lettuce leaves.

Ptcha (Calf's Foot Jelly)

2 calf's feet
2 onions, sliced
2 cloves garlic
3 quarts water
½ tablespoon salt
¾ teaspoon freshly ground pepper
4 hard-boiled eggs, sliced
3 tablespoons cider vinegar
2 tablespoons sugar
3 cloves garlic, minced

Have butcher chop calf's feet into small pieces. Wash in cold water, then in scalding water. Drain. Place in 3 quarts cold water along with sliced onions, and garlic. Boil 2-2½ hours until meat falls from bones. Reserve meat and discard bones.

To the liquid mixture, add meat pieces, salt, pepper, vinegar, sugar, garlic, and sliced hard-boiled eggs. Place in refrigerator and chill until jelled. Cut in squares and serve as an appetizer.

Gefilte Fish

2 pounds whitefish
2 pounds pike
2 pounds winter carp
4 large onions
2 quarts water
4 teaspoons salt
1½ teaspoons pepper
3 eggs
¾ cup ice water
½ teaspoon sugar
3 tablespoons matzo or cracker meal
3 carrots, sliced

Fillet the fish, reserving head, skin and bones. Combine head, skin, bones, and 3 sliced onions with 1 quart of water, 2 teaspoons salt and ¾ teaspoon pepper. Cook rapidly while preparing fish.

Grind the fish and remaining onion. Place in a chopping bowl and add the eggs, water, sugar, meal and remaining salt and pepper. Chop until *very* fine. Moisten hands; shape mixture into balls. Carefully

drop into fish stock. Add carrots and cover loosely and cook over low heat 1½ hours. Remove the cover for the last ½ hour. Cool fish slightly before removing to platter. Strain the stock over it, and arrange carrots around it. Chill. Serve with horseradish. Serves 12.

Roast Chicken

5-pound roasting chicken
2 small onions, minced
1 cup canned tomatoes
1 tablespoon chicken fat
½ cup water
1 clove garlic, minced
1 tablespoon salt
Pepper, paprika to taste

Place chicken in roasting pan, and cover with remaining ingredients which have been mixed together. Roast 2 hours in an uncovered pan at 325°, basting every 15 minutes to keep chicken from drying out.

Chicken Soup

Canned or dehydrated chicken soup may be used. If boiled chicken is served instead of roast chicken, use soup from boiled chicken. Chicken may be boiled and browned.

Prune and Potato Tzimmes

1 pound chuck
1 onion, sliced
6 medium white potatoes
1 large sweet potato
½ pound prunes
⅔ cup brown sugar
2 teaspoons salt
1½ tablespoons flour

Cover meat and onion with water and simmer for ½ hour. Add potatoes, fruit, and seasonings and simmer on a low flame for 1 hour longer. When tender, make a paste of the flour and a little water and add to stew to thicken. Serves 4-6.

Babka

1 teaspoon salt
14 egg yolks
3 yeast cakes
1 cup lukewarm milk
6 cups flour
¼ cup melted butter
1 cup sugar
¼ teaspoon almond extract
1 teaspoon vanilla
½ cup fine bread crumbs

Add salt to egg yolks and beat until lemon colored. Add yeast, milk and half the flour. Mix well and allow to stand until double in bulk. Add remaining flour, butter, sugar, and flavorings. Knead thoroughly. Let rise until double in bulk. Punch down and let rise again.

Butter a 10-inch tube pan, sprinkle with bread crumbs and fill with dough ⅓ full. Let rise about 1 hour and bake 40 minutes in 350° oven.

Sponge Cake

6 eggs, separated
1 cup sugar
1 teaspoon lemon juice
Rind of 1 lemon
1 cup cake flour
½ teaspoon baking powder
¼ teaspoon salt

Beat the egg yolks until lemon-colored and light, adding sugar little by little as you beat. Add lemon juice and rind, and cake flour which has been sifted twice with baking powder and salt. Beat egg whites until stiff but not dry and fold in.

Bake in tubular pan, which has been rubbed with flour, in a 325° oven for 45 minutes. When thoroughly cool, turn out onto a cake rack, inverting cake onto rack.

Chollent

This is the one-dish meal designed to meet the need for hot food on the Sabbath, when cooking is prohibited. It can be prepared the night before and allowed to simmer until the following day. Chollent is also called Shalet in some regions. Although the ingredients can be changed, the slow-cooking method gives the dish its characteristic flavor.

3 large onions, diced
2 tablespoons chicken fat
1 pound dried lima beans
  (soaked in cold water until tender)
12 medium potatoes, quartered
3 pounds chuck
3 tablespoons flour
Salt, pepper, paprika to taste

Sauté onions in hot chicken fat, using Dutch oven. When onions are brown, add the beans and potatoes, and place meat in the center. Mix flour and seasonings and sprinkle over top. Add boiling water to cover. Cover and cook over low heat for 3-4 hours. Transfer to oven and cook, covered, at 375° for ½ hour, adding a little additional water if necessary. Lower heat to 225° and allow to cook all day or overnight.

Rosh Hashonah

On this Jewish New Year holiday, it is customary to serve foods that will sweeten the year ahead. Apple, honey and carrot dishes in many versions are familiar to Jews from almost all national backgrounds.

Carrot Cake

1 cup carrot pulp
5 eggs, separated
1 cup sugar
1 pinch salt
1 teaspoon vanilla
1 cup walnuts, chopped
½ pint cream, whipped

Cook and strain carrots; squeeze dry. Mix egg yolks, sugar and salt and beat lightly. Stir in carrot pulp and fold in stiffly beaten egg whites. Add chopped nuts and vanilla. Bake in spring form 45 minutes in a 400° oven; cool. Serve with whipped cream.

15

Carrot Tzimmes

5 large carrots
5 medium white potatoes
3 medium sweet potatoes
3 pounds beef brisket
1 teaspoon salt
1/2 cup sugar
1 small onion (optional)
2 tablespoons flour
2 tablespoons chicken fat or
    vegetable shortening

Scrape and cut carrots into thin rounds. Pare and cut potatoes into 1-inch thick rounds. Sear the brisket of beef in pot to be used for cooking, turning frequently until evenly browned.

Add vegetables, salt and sugar. Add water to cover. Bring to a boil, then reduce and cook over low heat 2 1/2 to 3 hours, covered, until meat is tender enough to pierce with a fork. At end of cooking period, liquid should be reduced by half. If it reduces too quickly, add more water during cooking process. Do not stir contents of pot. To prevent possible sticking, shake the pot occasionally.

If an onion is used for additional flavor it should be left whole with 1 or 2 cuts at the root end to permit the flow of juice and should be removed before it becomes mushy.

When liquid has been reduced by half, turn into a baking pan or casserole. Add an *einbren* or thickening made by lightly browning flour in hot melted shortening and stirring in some of liquid from *tsimmes*. Shake the casserole to distribute thickening. Bake in oven for 30 minutes at 350° or until brown on top. Serves 6-8.

Prune and Apricot Tzimmes

2½ pounds chuck
2 tablespoons shortening
¾ cup tomato juice
Salt and pepper to taste
1 tablespoon sugar
6 white potatoes, quartered
3 sweet potatoes, sliced
2 cups dried prunes
¾ cup dried apricots

Brown chuck lightly in shortening. Add water to cover and cook 1 hour. Add tomato juice and remaining ingredients. Cover and simmer until tender. Add extra water if the stew appears to be drying out. Serves 4-6.

Teglach

Dough:

4 eggs
4 tablespoons oil
1 tablespoon sugar
2 cups flour
½ teaspoon baking powder

Honey:

1¼ pounds honey
3 tablespoons sugar
1 teaspoon ground ginger
1 teaspoon cinnamon
¼ cup water
½ pound filberts
½ pound pecans

Sift sugar, flour, and baking powder; add eggs, oil, to make soft dough. Roll into thick rope; cut into small pieces. Roll in the palm of the hand. Bake in shallow baking dish in 375° oven until brown — about 10 minutes.

Heat honey and the rest of the ingredients until they come to a boil. Drop dough and nuts into boiling syrup, cover and simmer for about 10 minutes, then uncover. Simmer slowly and keep stirring until all the honey is absorbed; then turn out on wet board. Form desired shape and let cool.

Eingemachts (Candied Radish)

Peel 2 large black radishes, and shred and cook in water to cover ½ hour. Bring 1 pound honey, 1 teaspoon cinnamon, and 1 heaping tablespoon ginger to a boil. Drain radishes and add to honey. Cook on medium flame, stirring constantly, until all honey is absorbed. Remove from flame and add walnuts. Serve as relish.

Honey Cake

3 eggs
1 cup sugar
1 cup honey
1 cup boiled coffee
2 tablespoons salad oil
3¼ cups flour
2 teaspoons baking powder
1 teaspoon each: soda, ginger,
   cinnamon, nutmeg
2 tablespoons nuts, chopped

Beat eggs well, adding sugar gradually. Mix honey and coffee; add oil and dry ingredients, sifted together. Add to beaten egg mixture. Reserve chopped nuts.

Sprinkle bottom of oiled pan with nuts. Pour in dough. Bake in 350° oven 40 minutes. If desired add ½ cup chopped nuts to dough.

Yeast Cake

½ pound butter
2 tablespoons sugar
Pinch salt
3 egg yolks
1 envelope yeast, dissolved in
   ¼ cup water
¼ cup milk
2½ cups sifted flour
3 egg whites
1 cup sugar
1 cup walnut meats, broken
½ cup raisins
Cinnamon

Cream the butter, add sugar and a pinch of salt. Separate eggs, and add the yolks which have been beaten until light in color. Then add yeast, which has been dissolved in lukewarm water, ¼ cup milk, and the sifted flour. Roll into a ball and wrap in waxed paper. Place in refrigerator overnight.

Next Day. Beat the egg whites until stiff, folding in 1 cup sugar when eggs are beaten. Remove dough from refrigerator and separate into 4 parts, rolling each part into a rectangle about 8 x 16 inches. Spread egg whites onto the dough, and sprinkle with walnuts, raisins and cinnamon. Roll as for a jelly roll, and place the 4 rolls on a baking sheet, cut side down. Allow to rise for 1 hour in a warm place. Bake at 325° for 25 minutes. Cool, and sprinkle with confectioners' sugar.

Yom Kippur

This is the High Holy Day, or the Day of Atonement. It is customary to fast for 24 hours, starting with sundown on the eve of Yom Kippur, and ending with sundown on the day of Yom Kippur. Highly spiced foods are therefore avoided the evening before, but the meal at the end of the fast may consist of the usual Sabbath or holiday dishes. Since this is a day of fasting, we will omit recipes that tantalize the appetite!

Sukkos

During the Feast of Harvest Huts, which recalls the first stopping place of the Hebrews in their flight from Egypt, fruits of the season and cabbage dishes are traditional in many lands.

Holishkes (Stuffed Cabbage)

1 large, fresh cabbage
2 pounds chuck, ground
1 cup rice, cooked
1 large onion, chopped
Sage, salt, pepper
2 small cans tomato paste
1 can tomatoes
3 tablespoons vinegar
2 tablespoons brown sugar
15 bay leaves
3 ginger snaps

Boil cabbage, head down, in covering water. Cook for 10 minutes, until slightly

tender. Separate leaves. Mix together chuck, rice, chopped onion, sage, salt, pepper, and about 3 teaspoons paste. Fill each cabbage leaf with a generous helping of the meat mixture, fold into envelopes, and lay in a large roasting pan. When cabbage leaves and meat have been used up, cover mixture with tomatoes, paste, 1 paste can of water, vinegar, brown sugar, bay leaves and ginger snaps. Cook covered for 3-4 hours. Serves 8.

Note: Stuffed cabbage benefits from being made the day before. Just re-heat when ready to serve. Raisins and prunes may be added to the above recipe.

Noodle Kugel

4 cups broad noodles, cooked
3 eggs
4 tablespoons brown sugar
1/8 teaspoon nutmeg
1/2 cup seedless white raisins
1/2 cup blanched almonds, sliced
1 tablespoon lemon juice
4 tablespoons melted butter
2 tablespoons bread crumbs

Cook noodles in boiling salted water till done. Drain. Beat eggs and brown sugar until fluffy. Add the nutmeg, noodles, raisins, almonds, lemon juice and melted butter. Turn into a well-greased ring mold or baking dish. Sprinkle with bread crumbs. Bake in a 375° oven 50 minutes or until browned.

Noodle Dairy Pudding

1 package medium broad noodles
1/2 teaspoon cinnamon
Salt
1/2 cup raisins
1/2 cup sugar
2 teaspoons almond extract
2 cups milk
3 eggs
1/4 pound butter

Boil noodles. Strain and run under cold water, to remove excess starch. Add cinnamon, salt, raisins, sugar, and extract. Add milk and eggs which have been beaten together. Melt 1/2 of butter, and add to mixture.

Put the remaining butter in the baking casserole. Heat the casserole and pour in the mixture. Bake in 350° oven until pudding is brown and crisp.

Apple Strudel

4 cups flour
1 teaspoon salt
1 egg
2 tablespoons vegetable oil
1½ cups lukewarm water

Put flour and salt into warm bowl. Make a well in center and put in egg and vegetable oil. Work into soft dough with water.

Knead dough on lightly floured board. Punch dough down on board at least 100 times. Knead again, not too much. Dough should be supple and silky. Place dough on floured platter and brush with vegetable oil and cover with an inverted warm bowl. Let stand 30 minutes to an hour.

Cover a kitchen table with cloth and dust whole surface with flour. Rub flour in with hands and put a little extra flour in center to start rolling. Roll out dough to 12 x 12 and brush with vegetable oil. Flour hands and pull dough out to cover table. Use the back of the hands for pulling and stretching. Pull dough over edge of table and cut off thick edge with scissors. Dry on table until dough feels like parchment, 10 to 12 minutes.

Filling:

Sprinkle cool melted butter over dough and cover whole of top with 2 cups bread crumbs mixed with 1½ sticks melted sweet butter, 1 cup sugar, 2 teaspoons cinnamon, 2 teaspoons nutmeg, ½ teaspoon allspice. Mix well and scatter over top of dough.

Spread 2 cans of pie apples over ⅓ of dough. Over the apples scatter 1 cup granulated sugar, 4 ounces chopped walnuts, 4 ounces blond raisins, 4 ounces black raisins and the grated rind of 1 lemon. Plump the raisins in brandy first, if desired. Fold a small section of dough over the apples to start the rolling. Pick up tablecloth and keep lifting to roll strudel over and over until entire strudel is rolled. Twist loose ends of dough to seal in ends and push in to close.

Roll onto a large buttered jelly roll pan. Bend strudel horseshoe style to fit into pan. Brush melted butter over top of strudel. Bake in 350° oven for 35 to 40 minutes. While baking, baste with butter. Serve warm or cold and dust with confectioners' sugar. This is a favorite dessert for Chanukah.

Polichinkas

2 egg yolks
2 tablespoons sugar
Pinch salt
1 cup sifted flour
¾ cup milk
2 egg whites
Apricot Jam
Powdered sugar

Beat together egg yolks, sugar, and salt. Add flour and milk and beat until smooth. Beat egg whites stiff and fold in. Batter should be thin. Pour on hot greased griddle, tipping so that batter will spread over bottom. Brown one side and turn and brown the other. When done, spread with a thick apricot jam. Roll up and sprinkle with powdered sugar. Other flavors of jam may be substituted, if desired.

Rote Grütze

1 ten-ounce package frozen raspberries
2 cups water
⅔ cup currant jelly
½ cup quick-cooking tapioca

In a saucepan, bring defrosted raspberries, 1½ cups water and jelly to a boil. Add tapioca to remaining ½ cup of water, stirring to mix, then add gradually to boiling fruit in saucepan. Cook 1 minute, stirring constantly. Pour pudding into bowl. Stir every few minutes until cool. Refrigerate until ready to serve. Serves 4-6.

Carrot and Nut Cake

3 eggs, separated
1/2 cup shortening
1 cup sugar
1 teaspoon lemon juice
1 cup carrots, grated
1/2 cup walnuts, chopped
1 cup flour
2 teaspoons baking powder
1/8 teaspoon salt

Beat egg yolks and sugar well and add shortening and lemon juice, beating until smooth. Add carrots and nuts, mixing thoroughly; gradually blend in flour, salt, and baking powder. Beat egg whites until stiff and fold into mixture. Bake in a greased tube pan in a 350° oven for 35 minutes or until done.

To remove cake from pan, invert tube pan on cake rack until cake is cool. Turn over and insert knife along sides of cake in pan, then invert again and tap until loosened.

Chanukah

The Feast of Lights celebrates the heroic battle of the Maccabees in 165 B.C. Potato pancakes are served in some lands, strudel (see page 28) in others, as symbols of homely endurance and sweet victory.

Potato Kugel

3 eggs
3 cups potatoes, grated and drained
1/3 cup potato flour
1/2 teaspoon baking powder
1 1/2 teaspoons salt
1 onion, grated
4 tablespoons melted butter or fat

Beat eggs until thick. Stir in remaining ingredients. Turn mixture into greased baking dish and bake at 350° for 1 hour, until browned. Serve hot.

Potato Latkes (Pancakes)

6 medium potatoes
1 onion, grated
2 eggs
1 teaspoon salt
¼ - ½ cup flour

Pare and grate potatoes and squeeze out liquid. Add remaining ingredients, mixing thoroughly. Fry pancakes, dropped from a spoon into hot shortening, until browned on the underside. Turn once and brown other side. Moderate heat should be used. When done, lift out and drain off excess fat on paper toweling.

Sour Cream Pancakes

1 cup milk
1 cup sour cream
1 cup flour
Scant teaspoon baking soda
Scant teaspoon salt

Mix all ingredients thoroughly. Drop batter by tablespoonsful onto a hot greased skillet, to make a very tiny thin tea-sized pancake. When brown on one side, turn and brown delicately on second side. Serve with confectioners' sugar, jam, or syrup as desired.

Kasha Varnitchkes

1 cup onions, chopped
⅓ cup butter or fat
2 cups kasha, cooked
3 cups broad noodles, cooked and drained
1½ teaspoons salt
Dash pepper

Sauté onions in butter or fat and combine with remaining ingredients. Toss together lightly and, if available, add *grebenes* which is a traditional ingredient for this holiday.

Grebenes (Cracklings)

Use fat and the fatty skin from chicken or goose. For each cup of fat to be rendered, use ¼ cup of sliced onions and 1 slice of apple. Wash and drain fat and cut in small pieces. Cook over low heat until the fat is almost melted. Add the onions and apple and cook until the onions brown. Cool and strain.

The onions and pieces of skin (*grebenes*—cracklings) can be stored in refrigerator separately from rendered fat. They make tasty tidbits.

Purim

The Feast of Esther commemorates the down-fall of the wicked Haman, head man of King Ahasuerus, by Mordecai, uncle of Esther the King's favorite Queen.

The Hamantash — Haman's hat — a three-cornered pastry, is made throughout Europe though Mediterranean Jews make donkey-ear shapes…"because Haman was a donkey."

Honeyed Nahit

2 cups chickpeas, soaked overnight
2 teaspoons salt
2 tablespoons melted butter
½ cup honey
½ cup water

Drain chickpeas, cover with fresh water and cook over medium heat for 1½ hours till done. Drain and place in a baking dish with remainder of ingredients. Bake at 350° for ½ hour.

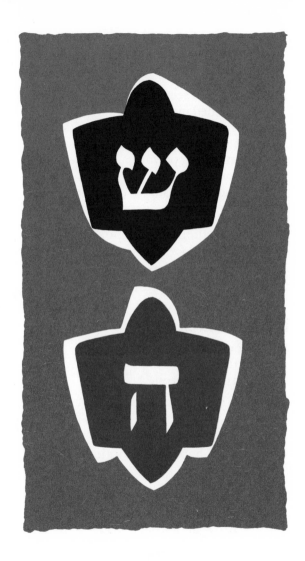

Poppy Seed Cookies

½ cup butter
½ cup sugar
1 cup fine poppy seeds, soaked in
   ½ cup scalded milk
1½ cups flour
Dash salt
1 teaspoon baking powder
¼ teaspoon cinnamon
1 cup currants or raisins

Cream butter and sugar and stir in rest of the ingredients. Add poppy seeds to batter and drop from teaspoon onto greased cookie sheet. Bake till lightly browned, at 350°, for about 20 minutes.

Hamantashen

2 cups flour
1 cup butter
½ pound cream cheese

Mohn Filling:
½ cup poppy seeds
1 cup walnuts, chopped fine
1 cup raisins, chopped fine (optional)
Honey

Sift flour. Cream butter and cheese together until well blended. Gradually add flour a little at a time. Make a ball of dough and put in refrigerator overnight. Roll out (not too thin), cut in 3-inch squares and fill with mohn filling.

To make filling, combine poppy seeds, nuts and raisins and mix with enough honey to hold together. Place 1 tablespoon of mixture on each square of dough and fold dough over to make a triangle. Bake in greased pan in 350° oven until cakes are golden brown, about 20 minutes.

Mandel Brot

1 cup sugar
1/4 cup oil
2 eggs, well beaten
1/4 teaspoon lemon extract
1/2 teaspoon vanilla
2 cups sifted flour
1/2 teaspoon salt
1 1/2 teaspoons baking powder
1/2 cup almonds, chopped

Mix sugar and oil together, and add eggs gradually. Add flavorings. Sift 1/2 cup flour over chopped almonds and add to above, then add balance of dry ingredients. Pat with floured hands into 2 long loaves (2 inches wide by 3/4 inch high.) Bake on cookie sheet in 325° oven for 30 minutes. Cut into slices 1/2 inch thick, when cool.

Passover

The Festival of Freedom marks the liberation of Israel from Egyptian bondage. Unleavened bread, or Matzo, is a staple everywhere among Jews, to symbolize the hardships of the flight and to constitute a reminder that the struggle for freedom is always difficult and full of deprivations.

Matzo Balls I

2 tablespoons chicken fat
2 eggs, slightly beaten
1/2 cup matzo meal
1 teaspoon salt
2 tablespoons soup stock or water

Mix fat and eggs together. Add matzo, salt and water. Place in refrigerator at least 20 minutes to set. Boil in 2 quarts salted water 30-40 minutes in a covered saucepan.

40

Matzo Balls II

2 eggs
1/3 cup water
1 teaspoon salt
1/4 tablespoon chicken fat
1 cup matzo meal

Beat first 3 ingredients lightly, and add chicken fat and matzo meal. Cover and chill in refrigerator at least 1 hour. Remove batter and with wet hands form into balls. Drop dumplings into salted boiling water. Cover and cook approximately 30 minutes or till done.

Many additions to the batter are possible including chopped marrow, parsley, liver, nuts or *grebenes*. (See page 35.)

Matzo Meal Pancakes

3 eggs
1 tablespoon sugar
1/2 cup matzo meal
1/2 cup water
1/2 teaspoon salt

Separate eggs. Add sugar to yolks and beat until very light. Blend matzo meal with water, and salt and add to the egg yolks. Beat whites until stiff and fold into rest of mixture. Drop by spoonsful into deep fat and fry until brown.

Matzo Brei

2 eggs
1/4 cup water
Dash salt and cinnamon
1 matzo

Beat together eggs, water, salt and cinnamon and break in 1 matzo. Allow matzo to soak in liquid about 10 minutes. Stir well and turn into a greased, well-heated frying pan. Cover and cook over moderate heat till browned on the under side.

Slide out onto a dish and invert into the frying pan to brown the other side. Serve hot, plain or with apple sauce, jam or sour cream.

Chremsel

1 cup matzo meal
1 teaspoon salt
2 tablespoons sugar

4 eggs, separated
2 cups milk or water

Mix together dry ingredients. Beat yolks, add milk and combine both mixtures. Let stand 1/2 hour to swell. Add beaten egg whites. Drop by tablespoonsful onto a hot greased griddle or frying pan in hot melted butter. Fry until brown on both sides.

Passover Sponge Cake

9 eggs, separated
1 cup sugar
½ cup sugar
½ cup matzo cake flour
½ cup potato flour

Beat yolks and 1 cup sugar until light and lemon yellow. Beat whites with ½ cup sugar until stiff. Sift matzo and potato flour together. Fold the flour and the egg whites alternately into yolk mixture.

If desired, flavor with citrus juice and finely grated lemon rind. Turn into ungreased 10-inch tube pan and bake at 325° for 1 hour. Invert after removal from oven; allow to cool before removing from pan.

Shavuos

The Feast of Weeks commemorates Moses' receiving the Torah and the Ten Command-

ments from the Lord on top of Mt. Sinai. It also celebrates the early wheat harvest. Dairy dishes are traditional.

Chopped Eggs and Onions

6 eggs, hard-boiled
½ cup onions, chopped
¾ teaspoon salt
¼ teaspoon white pepper
2 tablespoons chicken fat, rendered

Chop eggs and onions together until very fine. Season with salt, pepper and fat. Chill in refrigerator. Arrange on lettuce leaves. Serves 4.

Potatoes and Sour Cream

6 medium potatoes, pared
1 small onion, minced
Salt and pepper to taste
3 tablespoons butter
4 tablespoons sour cream

Cut the potatoes in cubes, and place in saucepan, add the onion, salt and pepper. Cover with boiling water and cook until tender. Drain. Add butter and sour cream and cover. Shake pan gently to coat potatoes evenly with cream. Serves 6.

Noodle and Cheese Cake

½ pound broad noodles, cooked
½ pound cottage cheese
½ pint sour cream
3 eggs
⅛ cup sugar
⅛ pound soft butter
Pinch salt

Combine all ingredients and pour into greased baking dish and bake 15 minutes at 400°, then 1 hour at 350°. Cut into squares. Serves 6.

Cheese Blintzes

Batter:

3 eggs
4 tablespoons flour
½ cup water
Pinch salt

Filling:

1 pound dry cottage cheese
2 eggs
2 tablespoons sugar
Dash cinnamon

Mix eggs, flour, water and salt to make a thin batter. Pour 2 to 3 tablespoons into greased frying pan, turning pan quickly so that batter covers whole area and makes a *thin* pancake. Fry until brown on under side only.

Mix filling ingredients together. Place a quantity of filling in center of each pancake. Roll and fold ends under. Fry again until brown on both sides. Serve with sour cream.

Rogelach

2 cups flour
½ pound butter
½ pound cream cheese
2 tablespoons cinnamon
6 tablespoons sugar
½ cup walnuts, chopped
½ cup raisins, chopped

Combine flour, butter and cheese, wrap in waxed paper, and leave in refrigerator overnight. Roll out dough on floured board, using a small amount at a time, to ¼ inch thickness. Cut with round medium cookie cutter. Roll each circle with rolling pin once again. Fill with mixture made of sugar, cinnamon, nuts and raisins. Roll as for a jelly roll and shape into a crescent. Bake at 375° on ungreased cookie sheets. When cool sprinkle with powdered sugar.

Favorite Jewish Dishes

Chopped Herring

2 herrings, (Matjes)
2 slices white bread
1 tablespoon vinegar
1 tablespoon water
2 sour apples
1 onion

Wash, skin and bone herring which has been soaked well overnight. Soak bread in vinegar and water until soft, and squeeze to remove superfluous liquid. Peel apples and onion and place all ingredients in chopping bowl and chop to a fine paste. Garnish with mashed yolk of a hard-boiled egg surrounded by chopped whites.

Kreplach

Filling:

1 tablespoon fat
½ pound meat, chopped
½ cup onions, chopped

Combine ingredients and sauté in skillet for 10 minutes, stirring frequently. Remove from heat and add salt and pepper to taste. Allow to cool before using.

Pastry:

2 cups flour
2 eggs
1 tablespoon water
½ teaspoon salt

Form into a ball, place on a floured board and knead till smooth and elastic. Cover dough with a bowl and allow to rest about one-half hour. Then roll dough thin and cut into 1-inch squares. Place a teaspoonful of filling on each square. Moisten edges of dough with a little water, fold over to form a triangle and press edges together to seal. The two corners at the base of the triangle may be pinched together to give the traditional form.

Cook in boiling salted water or in soup for about 20 minutes till the noodle paste is thoroughly cooked.

Meat Knishes

Dough:

3 large potatoes
2 eggs
Salt to taste
Enough flour to make dough workable
½ teaspoon baking powder

Boil potatoes in salted water. When done, mash and allow to cool. Add eggs and seasonings to taste. Mix well. Add enough flour to make a soft dough.

Filling:

2 onions, minced
¾ pound beef, cooked and ground
Salt and pepper to taste
Chicken fat

To make filling, saute the onions in fat until brown and add to the ground meat. Season to taste and add enough fat to hold mixture together.

Roll potato dough with floured hands into balls of desired size. Make a hole in the center of the ball and place a small amount of filling in the hole. Seal over the hole with more dough and pat the ball smooth. Fry in deep fat until golden brown. Size may be varied, if desired.

Pirogen

Pastry:

1½ cups flour
½ teaspoon salt
½ teaspoon baking powder
½ cup shortening
1 egg yolk
¼ cup water (approximately)

Filling:

1 onion, chopped
1 chicken liver, chopped
2 teaspoons chicken fat
1½ cups cooked meat, chopped
1 egg
½ teaspoon salt
¼ teaspoon pepper

Sift flour, salt and baking powder together. Work in shortening. Add egg yolk and just enough cold water to hold dough together. Roll out and cut into 4-inch squares. Fill each square with meat mixture and fold squares into triangles. Pinch edges together. Place in a greased pan and bake in 350° oven 20 minutes, until well baked and slightly brown.

To make filling, sauté onion and liver in chicken fat. Add to chopped meat. Add egg, salt and pepper and mix well.

Schav

1 pound schav (sour grass) shredded
2 onions, minced
2 quarts water
2 teaspoons salt
1 tablespoon lemon juice
4 tablespoons sugar
2 eggs

Combine first 4 ingredients and simmer for 45 minutes. Add lemon juice and sugar, and cook 10 minutes longer. Correct seasoning to taste. Beat 2 eggs in a bowl. Gradually add the soup, stirring constantly to prevent curdling. Serve either hot or cold.

Garnish with sour cream, and if desired, add diced cucumbers and scallions.

Borscht

10 large beets, peeled and diced
2½ quarts water
1 onion, minced
3 teaspoons salt
2 tablespoons sugar
¼ cup lemon juice
2 eggs

Combine first 5 ingredients in large kettle and simmer for 1 hour. Add ¼ cup lemon juice and correct seasoning to taste. Beat

2 eggs in a bowl and gradually add hot soup, stirring constantly to prevent curdling. Chill and serve with boiled potato. Garnish with sour cream.

Russian Cabbage Borscht

2 pounds soup meat
1 bunch beets
2 carrots
2 onions
3 stalks celery
1 green pepper
1 head cabbage
2 cans tomato paste
1 teaspoon sour salt
1 teaspoon salt
2 tablespoons sugar
1 cup sour cream (optional)

Boil enough water to more than cover meat. Add meat and cook fast for 10 minutes; then add vegetables, cut, not shredded, saving cabbage until later. Add at once sour salt, salt, and sugar. Boil 10 minutes, add tomato paste; continue boiling.

Cut up cabbage and add to mixture. Lower heat and boil gently 3 hours. While cooking, remove fat as it comes to the surface. Serve hot with sour cream (optional). The meat is excellent with horseradish.

Fried Herring

6 fillets of salt herring
1/2 cup dry bread crumbs
1/3 cup flour
1 egg
3 tablespoons light cream
6 tablespoons unsalted butter

Soak herring in water overnight. Drain. Mix the bread crumbs and flour on waxed paper. Beat the egg and cream together and dip the herring in the bread crumb mixture, the egg mixture and then again in the bread crumb mixture.

Melt 2 tablespoons of butter in a skillet. Brown the herring on both sides, adding butter as needed. Serves 4-6.

Kishke

2 feet beef-casing
3/4 cup sifted flour
1/3 cup matzo or cracker meal
1/4 cup onion, grated
1 teaspoon salt
1/8 teaspoon pepper
1/2 teaspoon paprika
3/4 cup chicken fat
2 small onions, sliced

Clean casing, scraping the inside. Cut casing in half and sew one end of each half. Mix well the flour, meal, grated onion, salt, pepper, paprika and ½ cup of fat. Stuff casings and sew open ends. Cook in boiled salted water 1 hour. Drain.

Spread the remaining fat and sliced onions in a baking dish. Arrange the kishke over it. Roast in a 350° oven 1½ hours, basting frequently. Serves 6.

Sweet and Sour Meat Balls

1 tablespoon lemon juice
2 tablespoons sugar
¾ cup water
1½ cups tomato purée
1 pound chuck, chopped
2 tablespoons onion, grated
1 egg
Salt, pepper

Make a sauce with lemon juice, sugar, water, and tomato purée. Heat in saucepan. Mix together remaining ingredients and shape into small balls, the size of large marbles; drop into the hot sauce. Cover pan and cook for 1 hour in a 350° oven. Serve as an appetizer, in a ramekin with *farfel* or rice.

Sweet and Sour Fish

8 slices whitefish, pike or salmon
3 onions, thinly sliced
3 lemons, sliced
½ cup brown sugar
¼ cup seedless raisins
1 bay leaf
2 teaspoons salt
2½ cups water
8 ginger snaps, crushed
½ cup cider vinegar
⅓ cup blanched almonds, sliced

Combine first 8 ingredients in saucepan. Cover and allow to simmer 30 minutes. Transfer fish to a platter. Add ginger snaps, vinegar and almonds to fish stock. Stir over low heat, until smooth. Pour over fish. Serve warm or cold. Serves 8.

Sweet and Sour Pot Roast

3-4 pounds brisket
2 large onions
1 clove garlic
½ cup clear vegetable stock
1 bay leaf
2 tablespoons vinegar
1 tablespoon dark brown sugar
2 tablespoons catsup
⅓ cup raisins

Brown brisket on all sides and add onions and garlic, sliced and browned. Add vegetable stock and bay leaf. Cover tightly and simmer 1 hour in Dutch oven. Add hot stock, if needed, from time to time, to prevent burning. Add vinegar and brown sugar. Cover and simmer another hour. Add catsup and raisins. Cover and cook ½ hour more until tender. Serves 6 to 8.

Sweet and Sour Tongue

1 pickled tongue (about 4-5 pounds)
2 tablespoons shortening
1 onion, chopped
½ cup brown sugar
½ teaspoon salt
¼ cup cider vinegar
4 ginger snaps, crushed
¼ cup seedless raisins
¼ cup almonds, blanched
1 lemon, sliced very thin

Place tongue in saucepan with water to cover. Bring to a boil and cook, covered, over medium heat for 3 hours, or until tender. Place tongue in cold water, drain and trim. Reserve 1½ cups of the stock.

Melt the shortening in a saucepan. Add the onion and sauté for 5 minutes, stirring frequently. Add the sugar, salt, vine-

59

gar, and stock. Cook over low heat for 5 minutes. Add ginger snaps, stirring until dissolved. Add raisins, almonds, and lemon. Cook over low heat for 10 minutes. Slice the tongue and serve with the sauce.

Kasha

1 egg, beaten
1 cup buckwheat groats
1 teaspoon salt
¼ cup shortening
2 cups water

Combine egg, groats and salt. In frying pan, melt shortening; stir in groat mixture and water. Boil. Cook, covered, over low heat 15 minutes. Serves 4.

Corn Kugel

1 can (No. 2) corn, whole kernels, drained
2 eggs
½ cup cracker meal
¼ cup milk (or sour cream)
1 teaspoon baking powder
¼ teaspoon salt
1 tablespoon melted fat or butter

Combine ingredients and bake in greased casserole 1 hour at 350°.

Egg Kichel

3 eggs
2 tablespoons sugar
1/4 teaspoon salt
1/2 teaspoon orange extract
1/2 teaspoon almond extract
2 cups sifted flour
1 1/2 teaspoons baking powder
1 1/2 teaspoons softened butter
Cinnamon sugar

Beat eggs until frothy. Beat in sugar, salt, and orange and almond extracts until creamy. Mix and sift flour and baking powder. Add butter and mix in with fingertips. If pastry is too soft to knead, sift in a little flour. Knead until smooth, about 10 minutes. Cover and set aside for 1 hour.

Divide dough into 3 parts. Roll out 1 part on lightly floured board to noodle thickness. Cut with a pastry wheel into strips 3/4 inch wide and 6 inches long. Knot or twist each strip. Repeat until all pastry is used.

Drop each knot into deep fat, 390 degrees. Remove from fat when golden brown and puffy. Drain on absorbent paper and cool. Dust with cinnamon sugar. Makes about 3 dozen.

Cheese Cake

¾ package zwieback
4 tablespoons melted butter
8 tablespoons sugar
1 pound cream cheese
1 teaspoon vanilla
¼ cup sifted flour
¼ teaspoon salt
4 eggs, separated
1 tablespoon lemon juice
1 cup heavy sweet or sour cream

Roll zwieback into crumbs, mix with melted butter and 1 tablespoon of sugar to make crust. Press crumb mixture on bottom of greased metal pan, 9 inches across and 2 inches deep. Or use spring form 9 inches in diameter.

Cream the cheese with vanilla, 3 tablespoons sugar, flour and salt, till fluffy. Beat egg yolks, add to cheese mixture and beat thoroughly. Add lemon juice and cream and blend well. Beat egg whites almost stiff, add remaining 4 tablespoons sugar and whip stiff. Fold into the cheese mixture. Pour into prepared pan and bake in a slow oven, 325°, 1½ hours, or till set in center. Cool in open oven, and chill in refrigerator before removing from pan. Serves 12.